INSCRIPTIONS FROM THE ATHENIAN AGORA

AMERICAN SCHOOL OF CLASSICAL STUDIES AT ATHENS
PRINCETON, NEW JERSEY
1966

1. Altar of the Twelve Gods

THE ALTAR of the Twelve Gods was at the heart of Athens. Herodotos tells us that it was the zero stone from which distances were measured, and an epigram found at the entrance to the Acropolis confirms this. The original altar was dedicated by the younger Peisistratos, son of the tyrant Hippias, in 522/1 B.C.

We know the identity of the sanctuary from the above inscription. The statue of Leagros son of Glaukon was set up at some time between 490 and 480 B.C. Fortunately its base was found in its original position, set against the wall of the sanctuary, and it is thus of the utmost importance in fixing one of the known monuments of the Ancient Agora to its precise location. 'Leagros son of Glaukon made the dedication / To the Twelve Gods.'

2. Base with the Marathon Epigrams

12. Praise of Sigeion

SIGEION, at the mouth of the Hellespont and on the southern shore, controlled one of the major trade routes of the Hellenic world, from the Aegean to the Euxine Sea. The text on this stone records an Athenian decree of 451/0 B.C. (the letters AN of the name of the archon Antidotos are visible near the break on the right edge of the stone in line 5) in which the Athenians extended a vote of praise to the citizens of Sigeion. The Athenians also promised to protect Sigeion from hostile attack by land, evidently a provision aimed at the Persian king whose threat to the neighboring Greek cities had been one of the reasons for the founding of the Delian Confederacy in 478/7 B.C. (10, 11). The city of Sigeion appears for the first time in the list of tributary cities of the Athenian Empire, paying cash, in 450/49 B.C.

THE HEROES OF PHYLE

13a.

In early winter of 404/3 B.C. seventy exiles left their haven of safety in Thebes with Thrasyboulos and occupied the mountain deme (parish) of Phyle. Their purpose was to rally the Athenians against the hated tyranny of the Thirty and to restore democratic government. They were besieged at Phyle but stood off the tyrants until they were strong enough (with added recruits) to move down from the mountain and capture the fortress of Mounychia. Athens was thus freed from military occupation, and later she gained complete constitutional freedom.

The liberators were honored by a special decree and were given each a crown of olive. As a group they were awarded a thousand drachmai for a sacrifice and dedication, and their names were inscribed on a stele of Pentelic marble together with the honorary decree and a laudatory epigram. Aischines, in his speech against Ktesiphon, quoted the epigram, and the initial letters of its four lines preserved on this stone (lower left) identify the inscription and its list of names. The names from the phyle Oineis (upper right) number three from Acharnai and at least five from Phyle. Since Acharnai as a deme was about ten times as populous as Phyle the high proportion of local patriots who were determined to return to their mountain deme is obvious.

13b.

14. Catalogue of Sacrifices

THESE religious sacrifices were inscribed at the end of the fifth century when the laws of Athens were recodified. They reflect the conservatism of the old social structure, naming as first sacrifices for every second year the victims for the festival of the 'Synoikia,' which celebrated the unification of Attica. The dates given are the 15th and 16th of the midsummer Athenian month Hekatombaion (clearly distinguishable just below the heavy groove on the stone). Theseus when king had brought the political units of all Attica together into one mother city of Athens. The citizens were classified in four phylai (tribes), each with its ritual tribal king. The phyle here responsible for the victims is named as Gleontes, though the kings of all the phylai shared in the perquisites of the first day's sacrifice. The herald also shared. Apparently they did not receive the actual meat of the lamb; this was sold and they received a monetary equivalent. Each phyle was divided into Thirds (or Trittyes), that of the Gleontes here named being the 'Trittys of the White Headbands.'

15. A Proxeny Decree

ATHENS strengthened her ties of friendship with neighboring states by honoring foreign citizens with the appellations of proxenos and benefactor. This beautifully cut text dates from the year 415/4 B.C. (the archon Charias is named in line 4) and is a typical example of this type of decree. The use of Ionic letters suggests that the man honored, who paid for the stone at his own expense, may have come from Ionia and Athenian relations with Ephesos at exactly this date suggest further that he was an Ephesian.

The diplomatic gesture failed to hold the wavering loyalty of Ephesos, which took advantage of Athens's preoccupation with Sicily to break away from the Empire and go over to Persia. Its defection must be dated earlier than 412 B.C. It has been suggested that the secretary's name (line 3) should be restored (Kle)ophrades and that he was a grandson of the famous potter.

16. Record of Public Auction

WHEN Alkibiades was charged with impiety and condemned *in absentia* his possessions, both real and personal, including slaves, were sold at public auction. His fellow conspirators in the Mutilation of the Herms and in the Profanation of the Eleusinian Mysteries suffered a like fate. The records of the auctioneers' sales were cut on stone slabs, which came to be known, even in antiquity, as the 'Attic Stelai.' They were at least eleven in number, probably a little over three feet wide and about five feet tall.

This fragment has been associated, because of the geological structure of its marble, with the stele arbitrarily known as the 'first' of these eleven. The items sold were himatia (mantles), sold individually and with prices and sales tax recorded. We do not know to which one of the conspirators they belonged. The date was after 415/4, probably 414/3 B.C. (see Picture Book 4, No. 7).

THIS small fragment of Pentelic marble belongs to the expense accounts of the Peloponnesian War in 432/1 B.C. It is something of a puzzle, for it cannot be placed accurately in the known text of these accounts preserved on other stones. The writing is characteristic—by the same hand—and there can be no doubt of the attribution. Moreover, the formulae are appropriate, that in line 2 recording a 'grant to the Hellenotamiai,' who handled the money that was borrowed from the Treasurers of Athena for purposes of war.

17. Peloponnesian War Loan

18. The Archonship of Pytharatos (271/0 B.C.)

THE WHOLE framework of chronology for the history of Athens depends on a knowledge of the sequence in office of the eponymous magistrates (archons). The Athenians are known to have kept and published such lists (5, above) and the annalists, like Diodoros of Sicily (age of Augustus), defined their years, in part, by naming the archons. Unfortunately the history of Diodoros is not preserved after 302/1 B.C., and the Parian Chronicle (an inscription which was composed in 264 B.C.) fails us at the same date. Dionysios of Halikarnassos, in his life of Deinarchos, carried the list of archons a little further down to 292/1 B.C. But for the Hellenistic Age the names and the chronological order of these eponymous magistrates must be recovered largely from the inscriptions.

A great step forward was the discovery by William S. Ferguson near the end of the last century that the secretaries whose names appear with those of the archons in dating decrees followed annually in the official order of the several phylai to which they belonged (Ferguson's Law). The secretary had his name in proper form with patronymic (father's name) and demotic (parish), and one could always deduce the phyle by knowing which demes belonged to each phyle. Much has been done in recent years to make the attributions of demes to phylai more nearly certain and to remove some sources of doubt and error.

Down through the third century B.C. there were thus long periods of time when the order of a series of archons might be known, but no fixed point could be determined independently to pin down the sequences to definitely dated years. For example, the archon Euthios was once dated tentatively, on general grounds, by Ferguson in 285/4 B.C. The secretary of his year was Nausimenes of Cholargos, a deme which belonged to the phyle Akamantis, seventh in the official order. The archon Ourias came two years later, for the secretary of his year was Euxenos of Aixone, and the deme Aixone belonged to the phyle Kekropis, ninth in the official order. But though the relationship was clear the definite dates were still uncertain. Over the last twenty-five years, for example, Euthios has been variously dated: in 287/6, 285/4, 284/3, or 283/2 B.C. What has been needed has been some external control. This could be effected if only the secretary were known, let us say, for the archonship of Pytharatos, for in his year the philosopher Epicurus died, and the year of Epicurus's death is known from Diogenes Laertios to have been the second of the 127th Olympiad, viz., 271/0.

This inscription has supplied the long-awaited evidence. The secretary of the year of Pytharatos was Isegoros, son of Isokrates, of Kephale (lines 3-4), and the deme Kephale belonged to the phyle Akamantis, seventh in the official order. The year of Euthios, therefore, also with a secretary from the phyle Akamantis, was exactly twelve years earlier (one complete cycle, there being twelve phylai at this date) and hence definitely 283/2 B.C. The epigraphical evidence is slowly bringing a precision hitherto unattainable into Hellenistic chronology, and though much is obscure much of importance is now better known, with repercussions down through the years depending on a better dating of the eponymous magistrates within the framework of the secretary cycle, which in turn depends on Ferguson's Law.

19. The Grain Buyers

THE *sitonai*, or grain buyers, were an official magistracy in Athens, as in a number of other Greek cities, in charge of the grain supply. In time of stress their function was of more than usual importance. Here the board of 247/6 B.C. (archon Diomedon) is praised for having done its duty with all proper care so that grain for the Demos (the Athenian Public) could be bought well and cheaply. This was soon after the end of the Chremonidean War and the fall of Athens to Antigonos Gonatas (261/0 B.C.).

But this text has another incidental interest for the calendar. The 17th day of the ninth prytany (the span of time when one of the phylai in the Council presided) was equated with the 9th day of the ninth month Elaphebolion. Since the year is otherwise known to have had twelve months only, just as there were twelve prytanies, it is clear that the one-to-one correspondence between day of month and day of prytany has been disturbed, apparently by the addition of days (up to 8 in number) somewhere in the months before Elaphebolion 9. Normally, Prytany IX 17 should have been (approximately) the same as Elaphebolion 17. But Elaphebolion was the month of the festival of the City Dionysia (see 20), and for some reason (perhaps bad weather) the authorities had to delay its celebration. Holding back the calendar by adding days or by counting some days more than once was one known way of doing this.

THIS is one of the twelve known fragments of a great list of victors in the lyric and dramatic contests held at the City Dionysia in Athens. The first fragment, which named the younger Sophokles with victories in 388/7 and 376/5 B.C., was discovered in 1835. The twelfth and last piece here shown, which gives the victory of his grandfather the famous tragic poet Sophokles in 448/7 B.C. and of his father Iophon in 436/5 B.C., was found on the north slope of the Areopagus in 1937. The name of Sophokles is broken, but can be read in part at the beginning of the second line of small letters.

This belongs to one of the most valuable documents bearing on the cultural history of classical Athens, which recorded, year by year, the names of the victors in tragedy, comedy, and lyric poetry from an epochal date which cannot now be determined well down toward the end of the fourth century.

20. Victors in the Theater

THE WELL preserved and beautifully inscribed stele 21 carried on both sides records of sales by the public auctioneers and probably dates from 342/1 B.C. The original stone carried four columns of text, of which part of the third and all (in width) of the fourth are here preserved. Broken though the third column is both it and the fourth give a poignant sidelight on stirring political events of the mid fourth century: the aftermath of charges and countercharges which followed the second embassy from the Greek states to Philip of Macedon in 346 B.C. This was the so-called 'False Embassy' which led to the peace with Philip known as the 'Peace of Philokrates.'

When Philip had overrun Phokis and established himself in central Greece the Athenians were bitterly divided about how best to deal with this menace to their freedom. This was the era of Demosthenes's famous *Philippics*. He was supported by Hypereides, destined himself to win a place in the oratorical Hall of Fame, whose indictment of Philokrates led to the latter's condemnation and to the confiscation of his property in 346 B.C. Demosthenes also attacked Aischines, both of them having been ambassadors, and failed of winning a conviction by only thirty votes out of a jury panel of 1501. The speech of Demosthenes in accusation and the speech of Aischines in defense are among our most eloquent heritages of Athenian oratory.

The inscription, as preserved, names Philokrates twice, for the first time about halfway down the left column and again in the sixth line of the right column, in the following contexts:

(1) – – – to be (confiscated all) these above-mentioned (properties of Philokrates, son) of Pythodoros, of Hagnous, (since Philokrates did not appear) for the trial (of the indictment to which) Hypereides had summoned him by laying information (before the Demos, but) was convicted *in absentia* in the (court – – – –).

(2) (– – – sold) in addition two workshops in (Melite, bounded on) the east by (a house) of Philokrates (of Hagnous, on the) west by a workshop of Hierokleides of Hermos, (on the north) by a house of Philokrates of Hagnous, and on the south by a road (leading from the sanctuary) of Herakles Alexikakos to the Agora. (The purchaser was) Hipponikos, son of Kallias, of Alopeke, the amount being fifteen hundred drachmai —all the properties of Philokrates, son of Pythodoros, (of Hagnous, being confiscated) since Philokrates did not appear for (the trial) according to the public indictment which was brought against (him) by Hypereides, son of Glaukippos, of Kollytos, but was convicted *in absentia* in the court.

Incidentally, the inscription confirms our knowledge that Melite was an industrial area in the city of Athens. It adds also the demotic of Kallias, a descendant of the wealthy and prominent ancestor of the fifth century who served as a kind of secretary of state for foreign affairs in the age of Perikles, when he negotiated a treaty with Persia (the Peace of Kallias in 449 B.C.) and a treaty with Sparta (the Thirty Years' Peace in 446 B.C.), as well as other treaties of 'perpetual friendship' with Leontinoi in Sicily and Rhegion in southern Italy somewhat earlier.

The inscription deals with a number of other cases of a nonpolitical nature, including failure to satisfy debts and failure to turn over to the state moneys collected as a public trust. Once convicted of default the defendant was liable, among other more serious disabilities, to twice the amount due, and his defalcation was inscribed in public on the Acropolis.

21. The Condemnation of Philokrates

22. Honors to Kephisodoros

THIS decree of 196/5 B.C. honors a prominent citizen Kephisodoros, whose tomb the traveller Pausanias saw just outside Athens on the Sacred Way in the second century after Christ. Pausanias describes his services to Athens: 'a popular leader and a most determined opponent of Philip, the son of Demetrios, king of Macedon. Kephisodoros induced to become allies of Athens two kings, Attalos the Mysian and Ptolemy the Egyptian, and, of independent peoples, the Aitolians and the islanders of Rhodes and Crete. But since the aid from Egypt, Mysia, and Crete was mostly delayed, and the Rhodians, whose strength lay only in their fleet, were of little avail against the Macedonian infantry, Kephisodoros sailed with other Athenians to Italy and begged help of the Romans. They sent a general with a force who so reduced the power of Philip and the Macedonians that afterwards Perseus, the son of Philip, lost his kingdom and was himself carried a prisoner to Italy.'

The Roman general Flamininus, as is well known, defeated Philip and the Macedonians at Kynoskephalai and then proclaimed the freedom of Greece at the Isthmian games in 196 B.C. Kephisodoros undoubtedly felt justified, some few months later, in asking and receiving exceptional honors from the city of Athens. This decree gives, in the fulsome language of eulogy, the motivation for his request: 'Inasmuch as Kephisodoros has on all occasions exerted strenuously his good will toward the Demos, has engaged honestly and incorruptibly in political life for nearly thirty years, and has never avoided either trouble or danger for the common welfare; and has performed all the liturgies to which the Demos appointed him, in particular serving well and honorably as Treasurer of the Military Funds and discharging the duties of stewardship of the grain fund with two colleagues in the years of Apollodoros (205/4) and Proxenides (204/3) respectively; has given advantageous laws for the concord of all Athenians; has advised sources of revenue that were fair and just; has explained how the Demos might keep firm in their faith existing friends and gain also others in addition; has foreseen the plots being prepared by outsiders and has set himself to oppose them; and has recommended good alliances advantageous to the Demos; and has gone on embassies of the greatest importance for the safety of the cities and the countryside; has contributed money and grain and many other gifts; has proposed many decrees that were useful, bringing glory and achievement and adornment to the Demos; has kept magnanimously to the same policy throughout; and by the continuity of his action and thought has been most particularly responsible, along with the good will of the gods, for the preservation by the Demos of its autonomy and for the conferment on many of the other Hellenes as well of the greatest blessings – – –.'

It can be said truly that a new era of prosperity began for Athens in 196 B.C. and lasted until the devastation by Sulla in 86 B.C. Kephisodoros was one of the architects of this revival.

23. A Boundary Stone

A BOUNDARY stone of the fourth century marks the 'Potters' Quarter.' It was found in place at the northwest corner of the excavated area of the Market Square, measured, studied, and photographed, and then buried again when the area in which it was discovered was filled in. Several other boundary stones of the same series have been found in place outside the Dipylon.

Another boundary stone (Picture Book 4, No. 35) proclaims 'I am a boundary stone of the Agora.' This was found in place east of the Tholos, marking the southwest corner of the Market Square. The shapes of its letters indicate its date in the late sixth century. Two other early boundary stones of the Agora have been found, but not in their original context.

THE BOUNDARY marker of the Sacred Street along which the ritual procession of the Pythais proceeded to Delphi was found in a late Roman level just west of the north end of the Stoa of Attalos. It dates from the fourth century and so is earlier by perhaps two hundred years than the stoa. It is quite probable that the Panathenaic Way, which ran in front of the stoa across the Agora, was used not only for the Panathenaic processions but also for the Pythaids, and that this street was named 'The Way to Delphi' when reference was made to it in connection with the worship of Apollo. It is clear from the epigraphical record that districts and streets in Athens were well named and marked.

Apollo himself had made the first journey along this road, and it was his route that the Athenians in their sacred embassies (Pythaids) always followed. The custom of sending such embassies goes back to remote antiquity, but the delegations that formed the Pythaids in the late second century were exceptionally festive and elaborate, and epigraphical records of them are preserved both at Athens and at Delphi.

24. The Sacred Way to Delphi

25. Demeter Azesia   26. Apollo Xanthos

TWO boundary stones of the fourth century mark the sanctuaries of Demeter Azesia and of Apollo Xanthos. They are mute testimony to the small shrines that existed unrecorded otherwise and largely unsung (Demeter Azesia is mentioned in a fragment of Sophokles) that must have been scattered throughout the city of Athens. The original location of neither shrine is known.

THE ILLUSTRATION on the opposite page, which appears also on the cover, shows the signature of the famous sculptor Praxiteles. It was carved on a facing of Pentelic marble which sheathed the base for two statues dedicated to Demeter and Kore in their sanctuary, the Eleusinion. The statues represented Spoudias of Aphidnai and his wife Kleiokrateia, daughter of Polyeuktos of Teithras. This Polyeuktos is known from the forty-first oration of Demosthenes, where the manuscripts give his deme (parish) as Thria. The inscription shows that this must be corrected; part of the demotic Teithrasios can be seen at the top of the photograph.

The statue of the husband Spoudias (line 3), who stood beside his wife, was not made by Praxiteles, but by another sculptor whose name cannot be recovered. Perhaps Spoudias, no matter who made his own likeness, was anxious to have the best possible representation of his wife and so commissioned the master to carve her likeness. The sculptor of Phryne and of Aphrodite herself was called upon to make the dedicated image of Kleiokrateia.

27. Statue Base

MORE Athenians are known by name than are the citizens of any other ancient state. There are already about thirty thousand known Athenians, and the number grows each day with new epigraphical discoveries. There are many lists, of various kinds. Soon after the re-establishment of democracy by Demetrios Poliorketes in 307/6 B.C. annual tablets were inscribed naming all 600 members of the Council (Boule), with patronymic and with deme.

This small fragment of Pentelic marble is part of one such list of the year 303/2 B.C. The men named are from the phyle Oineis, the first four marking the end of the large inland deme of Acharnai (twenty-two representatives out of the allotted fifty for the whole phyle) and the last three, plus others, are from the coastal deme of Thria between Athens and Eleusis. Thria may have had in this year a total complement of seven. Considerable portions of several such lists have been found in the Agora, and their prosopographical importance is of high order.

28. Roster of Councillors

THIS list comes from the late third century (*ca.* 215 B.C.). It exhibits a characteristic type of lettering in which, for example, the side strokes of alpha do not always meet in the apex at the top; this is called by some a 'disjointed' style.

The subject matter is one of the most common in Hellenistic Athenian decrees: praise of the prytaneis (councillors) of a given phyle for their good conduct while in office. The formulae are well known; they 'sacrificed all the fitting sacrifices on behalf of the Council and the Demos,' and performed all their other duties zealously and well. There were, in fact, two decrees, one of the Demos praising all the councillors of the phyle honored, and one of the Council praising the officers. The treasurer of the phyle was regularly named first, in this case Theophanes of Epieikidai, and the secretary of the phyle came second, here Sosias of Sypalettos. This type of 'honorary' decree was common until the time of Sulla, when the loss of democratic institutions caused a notable break in the epigraphical tradition.

29. Prytany List

30. The Laureion Mines

THE MINES at Laureion were one great source of wealth to the Athenian state. The silver from Maroneia was used to build the fleet that won the battle of Salamis, but little is known of their administration down through the fifth and early fourth centuries or of their actual revenue. Something can be learned from the inscriptions, for the mines were farmed out by the same officials (poletai) who sold confiscated property. Records were kept year by year, and in the fourth century at least were inscribed on stone and set up in the Agora.

The above fragment of Hymettian marble is part of one such record from mid fourth century. It names a mine, the Aphrodisiakon (line 5), which was bounded on the north by (property of) Demophilos (line 6) and which was leased to one Polymnestos (line 7). The record of another mine begins in line 8 and its bounds are given, one of them being (line 11) the 'road that leads to Laureion.' The preserved series of texts are invaluable in their topographical references to demes, districts, places, hills, gullies, roads, etc., and useful for the cartographer who wishes to study in detail the landscape of this southern tip of Attica.

31. Public Works

THIS document is part of the expense account of some public work. Mention is made of 'completion' or 'finishing off' and of salary and of the financial board of 'receivers.' These receivers (*apodektai*) make their last appearance in known records in 323/2 B.C., and indicate a date for this text earlier than the political upheaval of the Lamian war in 321/0 B.C., a date which agrees well with the character of the lettering.

As study of the documents from the Agora proceeds it has been possible to associate this fragment with others already known from the time of Lykourgos, known for his interest in public construction, but its exact significance is still not clear. Considerable sums of money were involved, for the last three lines seem to indicate a balance at the end of the year of some forty talents. A talent was six thousand drachmai, and a drachma roughly a daily wage.

THE GREAT library of Pantainos was situated just south of the Stoa of Attalos. Its dedicatory inscription has been preserved, showing that it belongs to the age of Trajan (A.D. 98–117). This was part of the 'University of Athens' and the center of philosophical study for many generations. The family of the dedicator, indeed, produced late in the second century another Pantainos, a Stoic like his grandfather, who was converted to Christianity and who became one of the teachers of Clement of Alexandria.

The library was, of course, the repository of books. The inscription here illustrated was found close to the dedicatory inscription of Pantainos and clearly contains regulations for the use of the library which bore his name: 'No book shall be taken out for we have sworn an oath. Open from the first hour until the sixth.' Problems of library management seem not to have changed greatly over the centuries in this vital matter of the custodian's duty to keep a firm control over the books under his charge.

32. Regulations of the Library of Pantainos

33. A Private Benefaction

A BRIEF item in the lexicon of Suidas tells of Akousilaos and his devotion to rhetoric. He was an Athenian who went to Rome under Galba (A.D. 68–69) and taught there. He prospered and at his death left a large sum of money to the Athenian people. It frequently happens that the literary texts help in the interpretation of inscriptions, but this is an instance in the reverse direction. The epigraphical text decides between two manuscript readings of Suidas for the amount of the bequest, confirming (line 3) that version which named the sum as 100,000 denarii.

The inscription also names the Attic deme of Akousilaos (Azenia, line 2) and gives the purpose of his grant of money as the purchase of real estate. The mention of Avidius Nigrinus (line 10), known to have been sent to Greece to settle a boundary dispute between Delphi and her neighbors, suggests a possible connection with the purchase of land provided for here.

THE PERSIANS were defeated at Marathon in 490 B.C., and the Athenians who died in that battle were given the signal honor of burial on the field. Their tomb is the famous 'Mound' which still stands as a memorial to them. In Athens itself another type of monument was erected. Its exact nature is much debated, and indeed this memorial of 490 B.C. can hardly have escaped destruction by the Persians when in 480 B.C. Athens was overrun by Xerxes. But the memorial was erected again with a new inscription, of which the first two lines here (2) form a part:

᾿Ανδρῶν τῶνδ᾿ ἀρετὴ [λάμψει φά]ος ἄφθι[τον] αἰεί,
[οἷς κἂν εἰ]ν ἔργ[οις ἐσθλὰ] νέμωσι θεοί·
ἔσχον γὰρ πεζοί τε [καὶ] ὠκυπόρων ἐπὶ νηῶν
῾Ελλά[δα μ]ὴ πᾶσαν δούλιον ἦμαρ ἰδεῖν.

The text is made out, with some restoration, with the help of another fragment of the same stone (not illustrated) and with the help of a fourth-century copy (3).

The valor of these men will shine as a light imperishable forever
   To whomsoever the gods may in future grant success in deeds of war,
   For they on foot and on swift-sailing ships
   Kept all Greece from seeing a day of slavery.

If the 'swift-sailing ships' carry some echo also of the reconstruction after Salamis, the second epigram (lines 3-4) refers exclusively to Marathon. It was probably the original text which stood on the destroyed memorial, deemed worthy to be repeated and added here as an appendix on a band dressed smooth across the decorative pebbling of the face of the base:

῏Ην ἄρα τοῖσ̣᾿ ἀδάμ[ας ἐν στήθεσι θυμὸς ὅτ᾿ αἰχμὴν
στῆσαμ πρόσθε πυλῶν ἀν[τία μυριάσιν]
ἀγχίαλομ πρῆσαι β[ουλευσαμένων ἐρικυδὲς]
ἄστυ βίαι Περσῶν κλινάμενο[ι στρατιάν].

These men had invincible courage in their hearts
   When they battled before the gates against countless foes,
Thwarting the army of the Persians who planned by might
   To burn their far-famed city by the sea.

3. Ancient Copy of an Epigram from the Persian Wars

4. The Tyrannicides Base

HARMODIOS and Aristogeiton were celebrated in song and story for their slaying of the 'tyrant' Hipparchos in 514 B.C. This revolt led ultimately to the democratic constitution of Athens in 508 B.C. Statues were erected to the tyrannicides, and their descendants were awarded maintenance in perpetuity at public expense. The first statues were carried away to Sousa by the Persians (though later returned) and a second group, of which this (probably) is part of the base, was erected when the Persian Wars were over. An ancient handbook on poetic meters preserves the first distich to show how the name Aristogeiton could be fitted into hexameter verse. This has made possible the identification of this small fragment:

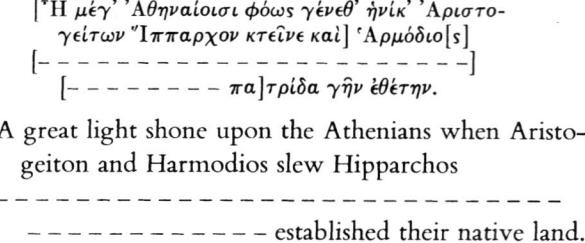

A great light shone upon the Athenians when Aristogeiton and Harmodios slew Hipparchos

– –

– – – – – – – – – – – – established their native land.

5. An Early Archon List

ABOUT the year 425 B.C. the Athenians inscribed on stone a list of their archons (annual magistrates who gave their names to the years and thereby dated Athenian inscriptions) from 683/2 B.C. down to that year. Several fragments of this list are now known, but this was the first to be identified. Easily rec-

ognizable are the names of Hippias, Kleisthenes, Miltiades, and Kalliades. Not so readily recognizable is the name of Peisistratos, in the last line of the fragment. These are all names from the golden age of the Peisistratid tyranny: Miltiades, the hero of Marathon, known from literary sources to have been archon in 524/3; Hippias, eldest son of Peisistratos, in 526/5; Kleisthenes, who later founded the democracy, in 525/4; and the younger Peisistratos, son of Hippias, in 522/1, who dedicated the famous altar to Pythian Apollo in memory of his archonship and the altar of the Twelve Gods (1).

6. The Argives who Fell at Tanagra

THIS text dates from 458 B.C. The Spartan armies inflicted a severe defeat on the Athenians and their Argive allies at Tanagra, and the monument to the Argive dead was set up in the Kerameikos at Athens. The lettering is in the Argive alphabet, and the names are arranged according to the Argive phylai (tribes). The first column, here shown, has the men of the phyle Hylleis.

After the heading in large letters is an elegiac couplet (not illustrated), possibly written by Pindar, which reads as follows:

[Τοί]δ' ἔθ[ανον Ταν]άγραι Λακ[εδαιμονίων ὑπὸ χερσ]ί,
πένθο[ς δ' ἔτλασαν γᾶς πέ]ρι μαρνάμ[ενοι].

These died at Tanagra by the hands of the Lakedaimonians;
They perished while fighting for their country.

7. A Gift to Athena from the Spoils of the Perisan Wars

THE ATHENIANS dedicated on the Acropolis a huge bronze statue which came to be known as the Athena Promachos, 'Athena the Defender.' It was made by Pheidias shortly before mid fifth century.

Overseers were in charge of the work, and their records of receipts and expenditures cover a period of at least nine years. The fragment of these records here shown records the purchase of copper and tin in considerable quantity. Ancient authorities tell us that the gleam of the statue could be seen from afar, and this resplendence would accord well with a high percentage of tin in the bronze alloy.

On other fragments (not illustrated here) there is mention of pay by the day, by the prytany (see below, 19), and for piecework. The overseers, their secretary, and their servant received regular wages. Among other items of expense in the making of the statue were the furnaces, charcoal, firewood, hair, possibly clay and wax, and silver for inlay.

8. The Building of the Propylaia

WORK on the monumental entrance gateway to the Acropolis was begun in 437 B.C. and carried on until the beginning of the Peloponnesian War in 432/1 B.C. The building was never finished, but in its perfection of workmanship and architectural splendor the Propylaia (as they are called) have excited the admiration of lovers of beauty throughout the ages and stand, even in ruins, as one of the noble heritages of the Age of Perikles. In the words of Plutarch, who praises the buildings of Periklean Athens: 'Each one of them, in its beauty, was even then and at once antique; but in the freshness of its vigor it is, even to the present day, recent and newly wrought.'

This small fragment gives, in the monetary units of drachmai and obols, some of the financial record of the fourth year, probably, of the construction.

9. The Treaty with Hermione

IN FOREIGN politics the sentiment in Athens blew hot and cold toward Sparta in mid fifth century. Kimon was of the pro-Lakedaimonian party which fell from favor in 461 B.C. Kimon himself was ostracized, but in 451 B.C. was again in power. He succeeded in making a five-year truce with Sparta and in renouncing a current and inconvenient treaty with Argos. The enmity of Argos toward Hermione and Hermione's staunch friendship with Sparta permitted an Athenian alliance at this time with Hermione, the beginning of which is here preserved in the form of an Athenian decree: 'Resolved by the Council and People - - -' (see Picture Book 4, No. 10). Hermione lay on the southern coast of the Argolid peninsula and later in the Peloponnesian War, whether hostile or friendly, was of strategic concern to Athens.

Leon, who moved the decree, was probably the man who moved the decree for Phaselis after the battle of the Eurymedon in 469 B.C. He played a part in Kimon's foreign policy similar to that of Kallias, after Kimon's death, in the foreign policy of Perikles (see 21, below).

THE TRIBUTE OF THE ATHENIAN EMPIRE

An alliance against Persia came into being under the leadership of Athens in 478/7 B.C. Its purpose was to lay waste the lands of the Great King in requital for damage suffered at his hands. After the organization of the Confederacy on the sacred island of Delos a board of Hellenic Treasurers (Hellenotamiai) was established and an annual levy of contributions was set at a total of 460 talents, to be paid partly in cash and partly in ships for naval service. The treasury was on Delos.

The Athenians soon became masters, rather than merely leaders. The treasury was moved to Athens in 454 B.C. and thereafter a quota of one mina from each talent of tribute (one sixtieth) was given to Athena. The annual records of this gift are known as the Tribute Lists.

In part of the list (10) for the thirty-third year (422/1 B.C.) the quota of Sigeion in the Hellespont amounted to 100 drachmai (H) and of Kyzikos, also in the Hellespontine district, to 2000 drachmai (XX). The names of some 675 tributaries are known, from Crete to the Black Sea and from the Aegean to Palestine. In 425/4 B.C. the total tribute was assessed at more than 1460 talents.

The lists of the quota to Athena from 454/3 to 440/39 B.C. were cut on the four sides of a tall stele of Pentelic marble (one fragment shown on the title page). The lists of the next eight years were cut on a second, somewhat smaller, stele. After that the records had separate annual stelai. Most of the fragments were found on the Acropolis, but some made their way to the lower slopes and have been found in the Agora excavations. Such a one is the small fragment (11) with numerals only. It belongs to the first large stele, and may be assigned to the list of the fourth year 451/0 B.C., where 200 drachmai represent the quota of the Thracian city of Spartolos.

11.

34. Gravestone

THIS grave stele of Pentelic marble of the first half of the fourth century B.C. is on display in the upper gallery of the Stoa of Attalos. It shows a bearded man of serene aspect carved on a sunken panel framed by pillars. He wears a broad-brimmed hat (petasos) held in place by a strap which passes over his hair to the back of his neck and carries a staff over his left shoulder. These are the accoutrements for a long journey. The relief owes its good preservation to its use as a paving slab, face down, in a Christian church. The lower fragment was found later and joined to the piece first discovered.

The epigram is characteristic in its Attic simplicity: 'Here lies Athenokles, a noble man, who excelled in good deeds and left many memorials of his virtue.'

35. A Christian Gravestone

THIS Christian tombstone was found in the center of the Market Square. The cross is unusually prominent, and the first six lines of the inscription were fitted in around it. The name of the departed (beginning of line 2) is lost. The text is not without its difficulties, but in the middle of line 4 there seems to be a phonetic spelling of the verb 'let him give,' that is, if anyone encroaches 'let him pay five gold pieces and suffer the magistrate's punishment.' Such threats of penalty for tampering with a tomb were common on gravestones in Christian times.

Title Page	I 4570	*Hesperia*, VII, 1938, p. 78.
1.	I 1597	*Hesperia*, Suppl. VIII, pp. 82–103.
2–3.	I 303 I 4256	*A.J.P.*, LXXXIII, 1962, pp. 296–297.
4.	I 3872	*Hesperia*, V, 1936, pp. 356–358.
5.	I 4120	*Hesperia*, VIII, 1939, pp. 59–65; XXXII, 1963, pp. 187–208.
6.	I 2006b	*Hesperia*, XXI, 1952, pp. 351–355.
7.	I 2228	*Hesperia*, V, 1936, pp. 362–376; XII, 1943, pp. 12–17.
8.	I 1137	*Hesperia*, VII, 1938, pp. 79–80.
9.	I 317	*Hesperia*, II, 1933, pp. 494–497.
10.	I 4809	*Hesperia*, VIII, 1939, pp. 54–59.
11.	I 4481	*Hesperia*, VII, 1938, p. 77.
12.	I 1276	*Hesperia*, V, 1936, pp. 360–362.
13.	I 16 & 18	*Hesperia*, X, 1941, pp. 284–295.
14.	I 727	*Hesperia*, IV, 1935, pp. 19–32; F. Sokolowski, *Lois sacrées des cités grecques*, Paris, 1962, pp. 27–31.
15.	I 1674	*Hesperia*, V, 1936, pp. 381–382.
16.	I 236cc	*Hesperia*, XXX, 1961, pp. 23–24.
17.	I 5880	*Hesperia*, XXX, 1961, p. 241.
18.	I 6664	*Hesperia*, XXIII, 1954, pp. 284–316.
19.	I 6064	*Hesperia*, XVII, 1948, pp. 3–4.
20.	I 4927	*Hesperia*, XII, 1943, pp. 1–11.
21.	I 1749	*Hesperia*, V, 1936, pp. 393–413.
22.	I 605	*Hesperia*, V, 1936, pp. 419–428.
23.	I 5770	*A.J.A.*, XLIII, 1939, p. 577; *Hesperia*, IX, 1940, p. 267.
24.	I 5476	*Hesperia*, XII, 1943, pp. 237–238; R. E. Wycherley, *Athenian Agora*, III, *Testimonia*, p. 119.
25.	I 513	*Hesperia*, IV, 1935, pp. 52–53.
26.	I 1454	*Hesperia*, X, 1941, p. 38.
27.	I 4165	*Hesperia*, XXVI, 1957, pp. 200–203.
28.	I 4720c	Unpublished.
29.	I 1860	*Hesperia*, Suppl. I, pp. 77–79.
30.	I 631f	*Hesperia*, XIX, 1950, pp. 210–218.
31.	I 3247	*Hesperia*, VI, 1937, pp. 456–457.
32.	I 2729	*Hesperia*, V, 1936, pp. 41–42; Suppl. VIII, pp. 268–272.
33.	I 6507	*Hesperia*, XXXII, 1963, pp. 24–25.
34.	I 3845	*A.J.A.*, XL, 1936, pp. 196–197; *I.G.*, II^2, 10593.
35.	I 1657	*Hesperia*, XVI, 1947, pp. 43–44.